THE BEAUTY OF
HORSES

THE BEAUTY OF
HORSES

EDITED BY DICK LIVINGSTON
PHOTOGRAPHY BY ROBERT & EUNICE PEARCY

JG
PRESS

Published in the USA 1995 by JG Press
Distributed by World Publications, Inc.

The JG Press imprint is a trademark of JG Press, Inc.
455 Somerset Avenue
North Dighton, MA 02764

Produced by
Brompton Books Corporation
15 Sherwood Place
Greenwich, Connecticut 06830

ISBN 1-57215-088-2

Printed in China

Edited and captioned by Bill Yenne
Designed by Ruth DeJauregui

Page 1: A pair of beautiful American Saddlebreds in distinctive red bridles.
Page 2: An owner poses proudly with her Appaloosa colt and Quarter Horse mare.
Below: A mare and her two colts kick up a cloud of dust. The horse is not only a beautiful animal, but graceful of motion and a joy to behold.

Note: Size measurements for horses given in this book are calculated in hands, which are the unit of measure tradi- tionally used by horsemen. A hand is equal to four inches, or 10.16 centimeters, and is used to measure the horse at the withers, or shoulder, which on a saddle horse is immediate- ly ahead of the saddle.

CONTENTS

INTRODUCTION

Below: This toddler loves to ride his pony.
Opposite: A pair of young riders in Britain preparing for a ride. Horses and riding are truly popular the world over.

Horses have been a partner with humans since the dawn of civilization. Indeed, this beautifully proportioned and intelligent animal has been present in our culture longer than any other domestic animal except the dog. Horses have served as beasts of burden or as mounts for riders for as much as four thousand years and continue to this day to be an important means of transportation throughout the world.

Horses are descended from the ancient, and now extinct, *eohippus*, or 'dawn horse,' that was found in many places on the Earth 30 million years ago, and which evolved into the modern horse, which was indigenous only to the Eastern Hemisphere. First domesticated on the vast steppes of Central Asia, the horse was adopted for use by peoples from China and India to North Africa and eventually Europe. Horses were adapted for a myriad of uses, from carrying soldiers in battle to pulling wagons and carrying heavy loads.

In the sixteenth century, horses were brought to the Western Hemisphere by the Spaniards. Native Americans, who had never seen such amazing animals, quickly realized their potential. Horses stolen from, or abandoned by, the Spaniards revolution-

Below: A group of mounted riders in the American West. Horses and horsemanship have been an integral part of the folklore and mythology of many cultures throughout the ages.

ized the lifestyle of the native peoples of North America's plains, prairies and desert Southwest. Horses made it possible to cover the vast distances of the American West in much shorter periods of time and they greatly aided the Native Americans in hunting the buffalo.

With the industrial revolution, many of the tasks previously done by horses — espe-cially in the fields of transportation and cargo hauling — were taken over by machines, but horses by no means became obsolete as an aid to humans.

Today, horses are still used to perform many tasks for which motorized vehicles are unsuited. On the great cattle and sheep ranches of Australia and North America, the use of people on horseback is still the pre-

ferred method of herding livestock. In areas of rugged terrain from Scotland to Alberta, people still use saddle horses on trails that are impassable to motor vehicles. Even the great draft horses that once were a common sight on farms, are still used occasionally.

In events from racing to rodeo, horses are part of sporting activities from China to Argentina. The Olympic Games include three individual and three team equestrian events. Horse racing is one of the highest paying sports in the world. In 1993, for example, Sea Hero took a purse of $735,900 for winning the Kentucky Derby.

Beyond their commercial and sporting uses, horses are trusted and useful companions to human beings, and objects of true beauty.

BREEDS OF HORSES

Below: *The Morgan is a popular riding breed whose heritage is traced to a single horse, known as Justin Morgan's Horse, or simply Justin Morgan, who was foaled in 1789.*
Opposite: *The American Saddlebred was developed as an all-purpose saddle horse.*

While most breeds of horses evolved naturally, many have been developed as a result of planning on the part of breeders. Some breeds have been developed by combining two or more breeds and selecting the better horses. People have long believed that like produces like; so, there has been a tendency to keep the better horses for breeding purposes. Thus, a type was developed by a group of animals having similar characteristics which distinguished them from other horses.

The breeds of horses usually developed because of their ability to perform some task useful to people. The draft breeds developed because of their ability to work, the Thoroughbred because of his running speed, the Quarter Horse because of his speed for a quarter of a mile, the Standardbred for his ability to trot or pace a mile in standard time, the American Saddle Horse for his easy riding gait and his style and beauty, and other breeds for some similar reason. The Tennessee Walking Horse was developed and named because of his ability to do the running walk.

The breeds were often given the name of the county or country in which they originated. Usually a name developed along with the

type and became the name of the breed. For example, the Morgan horse was given the name of the man who started the breed. Others were named because of their use, as the American Saddle Horse. Some types were never organized into a breed and lost their identity. When breeds of horses originally developed, there was often a lack of exact information as to the name and breeding of the early horses of the breed, so breed associations were formed after the breeds came into existence. When a group of breeders recognized that they had developed a type of horse worthy of perpetuating as a breed, a registry association was formed to keep a tabulated record of the horses. The earlier records had to be secured from the older breeders who remembered the earlier sires and dams. Sometimes there were conflicting statements and one still reads various contentions as to the origin of some breeds.

In North America, the original horses came from English, Dutch and Spanish stock, with the Spanish horses strongly influenced by North African types such as the Barb or Arabian. Later the improved and recognized breeds played a part in the mixing of the breeds that has influenced the horse of the West. Today there are those which can be considered purebreds, as well as various mixtures of breeds. A purebred is a horse whose ancestors have been recognized as a breed for several generations. A crossbred is a horse whose sire and dam are of different purebred breeds, and a grade usually means a horse that had one purebred parent and one of unknown or mixed breeding that may show distinct breed characteristics of one or more breeds. When one parent is predominantly of one breed the colt is said to be a grade of that breed.

Breeds of livestock have usually been based on a type of livestock which came into existence, and breeders of a certain type and color horse preserve the purity of the horses' breeding and eventually establish a breed. In color breeding, the breeds will be handicapped because fewer horses will qualify for

Below: Today, Arabian horses, descendants of the small, fast horses bred in North Africa and the Middle East for centuries, are popular both in their own right and as breeding stock.

breeding purposes than where there is no limitation on color. However, breeds often enjoy great popularity because of their uniform color. In some types and breeds based on color there may be a temptation to keep a sire because of his color. As a group of breeders were looking at a stallion of beautiful color, but poor conformation, they commented on the beautiful color of the horse, but reserved their criticism until out of the proud owner's hearing, when one person said, "It's strange what people will keep for a sire because of his color." So, in developing a breed, strict elimination of the undesirable horses will save the breeders of the future from having to overcome the mistakes of the present.

The light range horse is the accumulated result of the random breeding that occurs where many horses run at will on the open range or in large pastures. In an average group of range horses one will most often find horses resembling the Standardbred, Morgan, and Thoroughbred. Horses resem-

bling coach horses, Arabians, Quarter Horses and Palominos are found less frequently. Then there are some horses which, although small in size, show by their large heads, feet, and feather that they have a dash of the draft breeds. Percheron breeding shows more often than the other draft breeds. Also, in North America, some horses showing no particular breeding were traditionally classed as mustangs or cayuses.

It has been said that the best horses are produced in those regions that have the best soil. Good soil produces good vegetation containing the nutrients and minerals essential for the proper growth and development of horses. When horses are grown in a natural state they will reflect the limitations of the soil. Horses of the same breeding will vary with the region in which they are grown unless natural differences in the soil are equalized by feed and mineral supplements. Many times the difference in size is attributed to a difference in the breeds rather than

Below: Clydesdales are typical of the draft breeds, or work horses, that once served as an integral part of farm work throughout Europe and America. Today they are popular as members of demonstration teams.

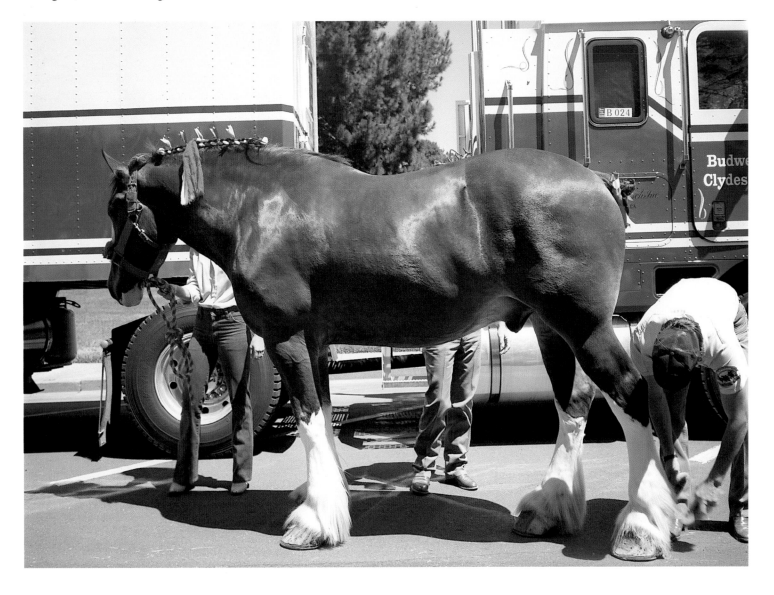

to the soil. This factor must be considered when studying the types of horses.

In the study of breeds, as in the training of horses, tolerance of another person's preference will develop a more congenial attitude among the breeders and help the common cause.

Among the fairly well established types are those largely distinguished by their color — such as the Palomino or Appaloosa — and others by their conformation and performance — such as the Morgan. Some of these types were becoming almost extinct until breed associations were formed.

The forming of breed associations has caused the ranchers to take more interest and pride in their horses. This interest has led to better horses, better care, better horse equipment, and better prices. Color is a very strong breed characteristic of some of the old established breeds. The Cleveland Bay is always bay. The Suffolk is always a chestnut. Certain breeds enjoy great popularity because of uniform color. The types that have recently been organized into associations may be classed as to color and performance. The color types are Albino, Appaloosa, Palomino and Pinto. The perfor-

Below: A young rider, proud of her buckskin colt.
Opposite: Enjoying a ride in the hills near Dolgellau in North Wales.

THE THOROUGHBRED

Developed in England with speed and agility in mind, the Thoroughbred is a beautiful running horse that originated after the change in the method of warfare from the knight in full armor to foot soldiers equipped with bows and arrows. A knight in full armor required a heavy war horse capable of carrying over four hundred pounds, but gradually tactics changed and the knight was replaced by the concept of fast and mobile calvary. The type of horse needed changed to one of speed and endurance so that the enemy might be surprised by swift and evasive action rather than brute force.

Throughout history there had been horse racing of some type, but the change from the heavy war horse to lighter, swifter horses stimulated the sport in England and Europe after the seventeenth century. At that time, there were many light breeds or types of horses in England but they were seen as being too small for riding horses. In order to increase the size, improve the type and escalate the speed of horses, the English began using the Arabian, Turk, and Barb stallions and mares. English horse owners and breeders took a great interest in improving the horses and laws were passed to discourage the breeding of smaller horses. They also obtained the light horses of the Middle East and North Africa to mate with the small mares of England.

Many histories of the Thoroughbred horse start with the statement that the breed devel-

Below: The magnificent Thoroughbred known as Just Kidding.
Opposite: A beautiful Thoroughbred mare and her colt.

oped from the Arabian, Barb and Turk. They cite the fact that Thoroughbreds can be traced to the Darley Arabian, the Byerly Turk and the Godolphin Arabian, sometimes called the Godolphin Barb. Historians neglect to state that the light mares of England to which these foundation Eastern sires were mated played an important part.

Some Eastern mares were imported, but the English mares seemed to predominate, so the foundation of the Thoroughbred was largely the result of mating imported stallions to native English mares, and in breeding the daughters of these matings to other imported stallions, or their sons, that had proven their merit.

While the male line means the very top side of the pedigree as son to sire to grandsire until the original recorded foundation sire is reached, the female line goes from daughter to dam to grandam until the taproot or foundation mare is reached.

Though the other Eastern mares had a part in developing the Thoroughbred, as time went on, their influence became less as the percentage of their blood occurring in a pedigree became less. However, the purity origin of the Thoroughbred has never been exact as to the purity of the breeding and the origin of the three foundation Eastern sires.

While the Thoroughbred horse does trace in the male line to the Darley Arabian, Byerly Turk and Godolphin Arabian, it has been said that the lines trace through three descendants of these stallions: Eclipse, the great-great grandson of the Darley Arabian; Herod, the great-great grandson of Byerly Turk; and Matchern, the grandson of Godolphin Arabian. Eclipse was born in 1764, Herod in 1758 and Matchern in 1748.

Byerly Turk was the charger of Captain Byerly during the Irish wars. He was foaled about 1679 and was in the stud in England as late as 1698. He was called a Turk because it was said that he was captured from the Turks. The Godolphin Arabian was foaled around 1724. He was about 15 hands tall. There are several stories of how he got to England. One story is that he was a present to Louis XIV of France from the Emperor of Morocco. Another story is that he was stolen and taken to Paris. An Englishman discovered him pulling a cart in Paris, bought him and sent him to England, where he became the property of the

Opposite: The conformation of the Thoroughbred is that of a powerful, yet graceful, animal built for speed. Thoroughbreds also enjoy running.

Earl of Godolphin. Some argue that he was a Barb. The Darley Arabian has a more definite history. He was bought in Aleppo by Thomas Darley, who sent him to his father in England. He arrived in England in 1704, at the age of four. He, too, is said to have stood about 15 hands high.

All of the Eastern horses of that time had some similar characteristics. The horses were exchanged among the Eastern people so it is possible that the horses were said to be of the breed that predominated in the country from which they came. The Arabian horses were being bred prior to the seventeenth century on the Arabian peninsula by the Bedouins. The early Arabians were about 14.2 hands tall and weighed 800 to 950 pounds. The Arabians were the best looking of the three Eastern breeds. They had beautiful heads, fine dense bone and short backs. They were noted for their ability to carry great weight for long distances.

The Barb originated on the Barbary Coast in North Africa in what is now Tunisia, Algeria and Morocco. From here, many were taken to Spain by the Moors. They were approximately the same size as the

Below: *A pair of Thoroughbred owners and their stock enjoy a relaxed moment after the race.*

Arabian, but they were plainer. The Turk was a mixture of the breeds of Asia. Standing 15 to 16 hands tall, they were larger than the other breeds, and resembled the present Thoroughbred.

The foundation mares of the Thoroughbred were also few. Originally there were about 100 foundation mares, but this number has decreased to less than half.

The Thoroughbred has been bred for performance for three centuries. The fastest have been mated to the fastest whenever possible with the preference on speed. Thus, in terms of showing, they have not really been a show breed except in those classes where performance counted for more than conformation and breed characteristics. In a few classes they are judged for conformation and breed characteristics but breeders tend to mate their mares to stallions that can run, rather than to those that have won show ribbons.

The history of the Thoroughbred in North America is only slightly different from that of England, but this difference traditionally excluded many American Thoroughbreds from registration in the General Stud Book of England. All male lines of American Thoroughbreds go back to Eclipse, Herod

Below: A Thoroughbred mare and her foal regard one another across the fence.

and Matchern, just as is the case with all English Thoroughbreds. However, there are some female families recognized in the American Stud Book that are not recognized by the General Stud Book of England. The American lines or families were recognized until 1913, when the Jersey Act was introduced. This was an act of the Stewarts of the English Jockey Club that stated that only those Thoroughbreds that traced to certain tap-root mares of England would be permitted to be registered in the English General Stud Book. The act is named the Jersey Act after Lord Jersey. As some of the best Thoroughbreds in America trace to tap-root mares registered only in the American Stud Book they can be registered in the American Stud Book, but not in the General Stud Book of England.

The American colonies were settled during the time that the Thoroughbred of England was developing into a breed, and there were informal races and matched races in practically all of the colonies. There was racing on Long Island in 1665, in the Carolinas in 1734 and in Virginia in 1745.

The horses were not registered, but many were closely related to the horses that raced in England. Rulle Rock, one of the earliest Thoroughbreds to come to America, was imported in 1730 before the breed was definitely formed, but he was 21 years old and had little influence on the Thoroughbred of America.

After 1745, more Thoroughbreds or horses related to the horses that developed the Thoroughbred breed were imported and some of them formed the foundation of the American Thoroughbred. After the Revolution, many more were imported. These were mated with American bred mares and stallions that had raced in America.

In 1791 James Weatherby, Jr published an Introduction to a General Stud Book. This book was published in England. He drew his material from publications that had been published in connection with racing, and from private sources. First published in 1793, it has been revised several times. The American Stud Book was published in 1873 by Samuel D Bruce.

Thoroughbreds were introduced into western North America by English stockmen

Opposite: The rewards of Thoroughbred ownership are many, not the least of which is the companionship of a truly great animal.

who brought their favorite breed with them. These horses were mixed with other breeds and lost their identity. However, many stockmen of the West have always liked fast horses and have kept some Thoroughbreds pure for racing. The use of Thoroughbred stallions almost exclusively by the American Remount Association in the early twentieth century greatly increased the number of grade Thoroughbred horses and some were trained for polo and sold in the eastern states.

Today, there are well over a half million Thoroughbreds in the United States alone, making it the third most common breed after the American Quarter Horse and the Arabian. While the other breeds have increased in numbers as sires of grade horses, the registered Thoroughbreds have increased in number in purebred stables.

Bred for speed, Thoroughbreds vary in size from 14.2 to 17 hands and from 850 to 1350 pounds. The most common colors are bay, chestnut and brown. They are a deep chested, narrow and light boned breed. Their muscles have developed such strength that the fine joints cannot always stand the strain, and some go unsound from straining their tendons and joints.

It has been said that few breeds have more courage, or 'heart' as horsemen say. Thoroughbreds have the will to keep on running under the most adverse conditions, and some have been known to finish races although badly crippled. For this reason the trainer of Thoroughbreds must be careful in the use of force in training. Their great resistance and quick and sudden action can cause them to injure themselves.

The sprinters or short distance racers are likely to have bodies that are longer than their height at the withers. They have shorter and thicker muscles than the long distance runners.

They are a natural galloping horse. Their gallop is long, straight, and free, but not high. They are often criticized as pleasure riding horses because they lack flexion and height of action at the walk and trot. All excessive height of action has been eliminated for the sake of speed. They are the most perfect and fastest running horses, and because of this ability are used in races and sports where speed is essential.

Right: *Perhaps the greatest Thoroughbred of modern times, Secretariat achieved immortality in 1973, by winning the Triple Crown, with record times posted in two of the three races.*

Sired by Bold Ruler and foaled by Something Royal, Secretariat was born on 10 March 1970 and had a respectable season as a two-year-old. By May 1973, he was a highly regarded race horse, though his true promise was to be demonstrated on 5 May with the 99th running of the Kentucky Derby, in which he became the first horse in history to post a time of less than two minutes.

He went on to win both the Preakness and the Belmont Stakes by setting track records. At Belmont, he finished 20 lengths ahead of the rest of the pack.

Below: *A young Thoroughbred in training. They display an instinctive eagerness to run.*

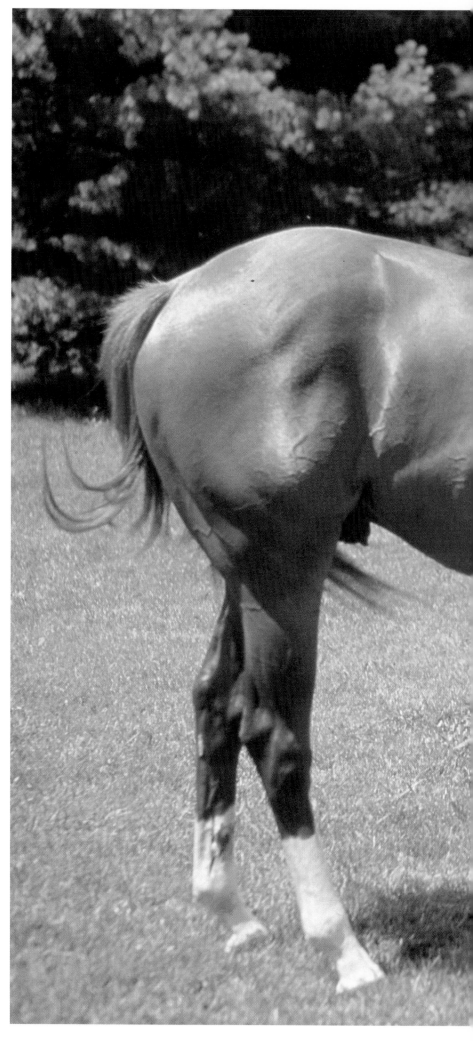

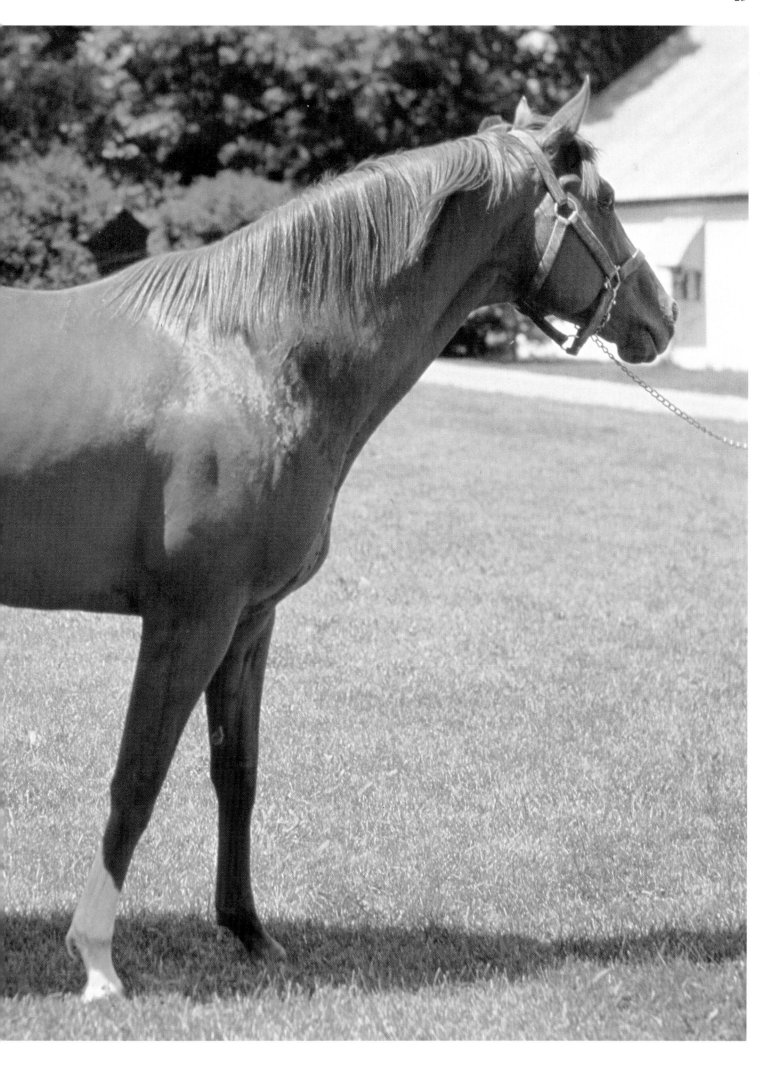

THE ARABIAN

One of the most beautiful of all horses, the Arabian originated in western Asia and has been bred by the Bedouins of the Middle East and the Arabian peninsula for over a thousand years. With distinctive heads, fine, dense bones and short backs, they were noted for their ability to carry great weight for long distances. The Arabian is usually recognized as one of the oldest purebred breed of horses. There are many stories concerning their origin, and the Arabian is one of the foundation breeds of most of the breeds of light horses and some of the draft breeds. The Arabian and Barb are remotely related to the wild mustangs of America through the Spanish horse.

A small horse, Arabians are thought to have originally stood about 14.2 hands, weighing 800 to 950 pounds. Today, however, some American breeders, through selection and heavy feeding, are developing them into larger horses that may stand over 15

hands and weigh 1000 pounds. The Arabian is very prominent in the United States, where it numbers almost 700,000 and is the second most populous breed. There are also a large number of cross-breeds with a sizable percentage of Arabian blood. Breeds of horses that have a great deal of Arabian breeding are often thought of as being high strung and lacking in calmness of disposition, but people who have owned or used Arabian horses are quite generous in their praise of their intelligence, endurance, beauty, and usefulness. Arabian horses are usually good walkers, fair trotters, and excellent gallopers, quite fast for short distances. Since the middle of the twentieth century, the Arabian horse has become very popular in California and the American Southwest. Shows of the attractive and well-trained Arabian horses have done a great deal to popularize the breed.

In color, Arabians may be gray, bay, chestnut, or brown. Pure blacks and whites are rarely found. Spotted horses do not occur in pure Arabian horses, but when crossed with other breeds, spotted colors may occur. Arabians are usually marked with white

Below: A young Arabian stallion, bridled and ready to go.
***Opposite:** A pair of young Arabians.*

about the face and legs. They are very beautiful and have a great deal of style, finish, and quality.

The head of the Arabian horse is especially attractive, being clean cut and tapering from the eyes to the muzzle, with a slight dish in the face, prominent eyes, and short ears. The head is neatly attached to a long, slender, well arched neck. They have one fewer vertebra than most horses, which gives them a short back suitable for weight carrying. The croup is long and level. The short, well-carried tail has one or two fewer vertebra than most other breeds. The legs and feet of Arabian horses are excellent, the knee and hock joints large and strong, the cannon bone short and dense, and the hoof strong and dense. The Arabians are a remarkably sound breed and possess both endurance and durability.

Below: A three-year-old Arabian stallion rests in his stable at the end of a long day.

Opposite: An Arabian mare and her foal at an an Arabian horse ranch in California.

Overleaf: A classic view of a magnificent Arabian stallion.

THE QUARTER HORSE

Below: A magnificent mare with a beautiful silver bridle.
Opposite: A Quarter Horse mare poses protectively with her colt.

The most common of North American breeds, the Quarter Horse numbers nearly two million. Though Quarter Horses are often associated with Texas and the West, the origin of the breed was in Virginia and other Colonial states. The early horses of the Colonial settlers came from England and these were crossed with the Spanish horse or the Native American ponies that descended from Spanish stock. The result was a compact, heavy muscled horse that could run exceedingly fast for a short distance that tended to resemble the early Thoroughbreds. Indeed, the Quarter Horse name was used because of their speed for a quarter of a mile.

Another early name for the breed was 'Steeldust,' a name that is said to have originated with horses of the Quarter Horse type bred in or around the Texas counties of Travis, Gonzales and Frio. According to legend, Steeldust, a Thoroughbred stallion, was taken to McKinney, Texas in 1849. Some stories are that he won fame by winning a matched race, and others that he lost by default. At any rate, he was used extensively as a sire and his blood spread to many cow ponies in Texas through grade offspring.

Below: The Quarter Horse has been bred over the years to become one of the best all-around horses for riding.
Opposite: This young Quarter Horse colt is obviously ready for action.

Another set of legends is cited to explain how Quarter Horses were once known as 'Billy' horses. In one story, a man named William Flemming is said to have brought a colt from Kentucky to Gonzales, Texas, soon after the Civil War. The colt was said to be a descendant of Steeldust. The colt was called Billy and his offspring became known as Billy Horses. Billy was described as being 14.3 hands and weighing 1000 pounds. His body was deep and heavy, his hips sloping, legs short, and his short neck was carried low. Another story of Billy Horses is that Billy Blanton, a gambler, brought to Tampico, Mexico, a Spanish stallion and a mare from Spain. The mare was a dappled brown named Paisano and the stallion was a

sorrel named Whalebone. A pair of descendants of Paisano and Whalebone were taken to Texas in the late 1870s and produced eight colts that were very fast. Their descendants were called Billy Horses from the name of Billy Blanton. This strain is also recognized as a Quarter Horse type. The term Billy has a more limited use than Steeldust or Quarter Horse.

A major influence upon the Quarter Horse was the Spanish Horse. Most of the early horses of the American Southwest were descendants of the Spanish horses, which were themselves descendants of horses developed in the West Indies before being taken to mainland Mexico and what is now the United States. The Spanish Horses are, in

turn, thought to have descended from Arabians or Barbs. However it is doubtful that the best horses of Spain were sent to mount the soldier and explorer in the New World.

At first, the Native Americans were afraid of the horses and the Spaniards were able to exert a great influence over the Native Americans because of their mounted soldiers. As some of the horses used on various expeditions were lost or taken as spoils of war, they gradually came into use by the Native Americans. Meanwhile, in Texas,

Below and opposite: A white blaze, such as we see on these youngsters, is a common characteristic among Quarter Horses.

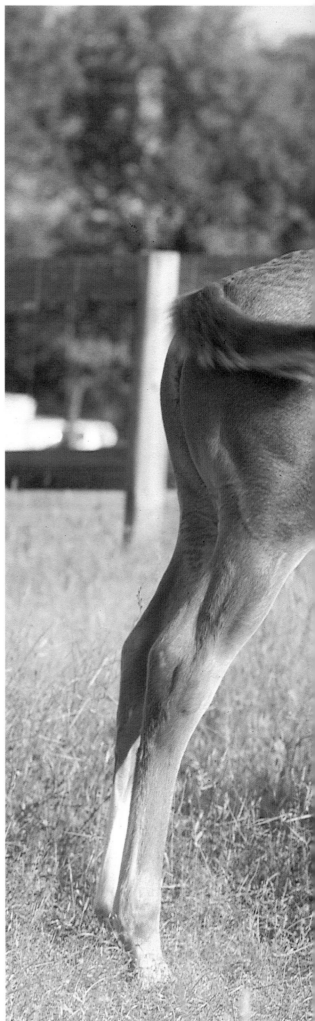

New Mexico and California, some Native Americans worked on the mission ranches and were taught to ride horses. These Native Americans often returned to their tribes and taught others to ride and manage horses. The Native Americans quickly learned to master their animals and began to use them in their hunts and wars. The Native Americans often looked upon the horse as an animal for food as well as an animal of burden. This gave them an advantage in war, as they could always have a source of food after the pursuing soldiers were forced to give up the chase because of a lack of food.

Between 1680 and 1693, as the Native Americans fought with the Spanish stationed at the missions in New Mexico, they took many of their horses. These horses by various means drifted into the hands of traders and trappers, and some became the property of the French, who secured most of their horses from the Native Americans and Spaniards. These horses generally came to be known as Spanish Horses and evolved into a sort of

independent breed that ultimately influenced other breeds, such as the Quarter Horse.

Some particularly pure Spanish horses were developed in lower California where they were isolated from outside influences. California was well settled by the Spanish when the Americans arrived and the missions and ranches had some excellent horses, and the geldings or stallions were used for working their vast herds of cattle. Meanwhile, the Spanish missions and settlers east of the Mississippi River helped to scatter the Spanish horses in the southeastern states, and Spanish horses from the West Indies found their way into the colonies of the Atlantic seaboard. However, they did not exert as much influence on those horses as on those of the Southwest.

After the Quarter Horse became established in the latter part of the nineteenth century, they were bred among themselves and the type became almost as definite as a breed. This type spread to all the western states — especially Arizona and New

Below: A young Quarter Horse foal.
Opposite: This Quarter Horse, bridled and about to be saddled, thoughtfully eyes the camera.

Mexico — and to the western provinces, such as Alberta. It is claimed that three Quarter Horses, named Bob Wade, Judge Thomas, and San F, made records of 21.25 seconds for a quarter mile on a straight course. Bob Wade made his record in Butte, Montana, in 1890 at the age of four while carrying 122 pounds.

Soon after the advent of Quarter Horses into Texas the huge cattle herds started up the trails for the western range or northern markets. The great cattle drives of the 1860s and 1870s — which hit their peak in 1871 with 700,000 head of Longhorn cattle — required the services of literally thousands of cowboys to serve as drovers. The Quarter Horse, along with the Spanish horses, were ideal as mounts for the cowboys working the herds. The type of work called for speed, endurance, durability and 'cow sense.' The Quarter Horse met these requirements.

Below: A strikingly beautiful, almost black, Quarter Horse at a ranch near Austin, Texas. Quarter Horses this color are not as common as lighter shades.
Opposite: *In terms of color, a buckskin coat with a black tail and mane can be a very beautiful combination.*

When the herds went up the trails to Kansas, Montana, Wyoming, and Colorado, remudas of horses were sometimes taken along and sold at the destination along with the cattle. These horses helped to populate the western states with horses and influence the horses that were largely of Spanish ancestry. The southwestern states were less in line of the western immigration following the gold rush in 1849 and the settlement of Utah and Oregon. So the horses of the Southwest had less chance of becoming mixed with the other breeds of horses than the horses of the states farther north. There must have been some mixing of the breeds of horses in Texas, for many settlers, soldiers, trappers, and traders went into Texas from other states and they usually took a few

Below: A Quarter Horse mare and her foal perk up their ears.
Opposite: This buckskin-colored Quarter Horse is ready to be ridden.

horses with them. No doubt these horses had their influence on improving some of the Texas horses that later went up the cattle trails. Regardless of this, the old Spanish horses were largely the foundation horses of the western states, although the Quarter Horse developed from them through selective breeding and in order to accentuate desirable traits.

During breaks from the cattle drives, the cowboys often matched their horses for short races, and the desire for a horse that could outrun all comers along the trail influenced the selection of the breeding stock that solidly established the Quarter Horse. The fast mares were bred to the fast stallions. Thus speed as well as ability to work cattle was combined in the same horse. It is remarkable that the Quarter Horse remained practically pure in breeding for so many years. They were kept as a definite type because cattlemen needed horses of their ability. So they continued as a type when there was no breed Association to register and promote them as a breed.

After the turn of the century, when polo was in its infancy in the United States, many Quarter Horses were used for playing polo. The change in the game that came in the 1930s, which allowed larger horses to be used, changed the demand more toward the pure Thoroughbred type. In 1939 a group of horsemen met at the Fort Worth Stock Show to discuss forming an Association, and in March 1940, the American Quarter Horse Association was formed. Within a short time rules and regulations were drawn up and the registration of Quarter Horses began.

It is an interesting testimony to the importance of the Quarter Horse that at the close of the twentieth century, the majority of them are still at work on the vast cattle ranches of the West, just as they were at the close of the nineteenth century. One is reminded here of the Great Trail Drive held in 1989 to celebrate the centennial of Montana's statehood, a cattle drive that was attended by hundreds of working cowboys on Quarter Horses. Quarter Horses are also the horse of choice of rodeo cowboys.

Below: A fine-featured chestnut Quarter Horse.
Opposite: A playful Quarter Horse foal.
Overleaf: A fine view of a beautifully-formed Quarter Horse mare.

OTHER SADDLE HORSE BREEDS

Below: A fine view of an American Saddlebred. Opposite: A buckskin-colored American Saddle Horse stallion.

The American Saddle Horse, or American Saddlebred, developed in the states of Kentucky, Missouri, Tennessee, Virginia, and surrounding states in the eighteenth century for an easy riding horse to be used on the rough trails and poor roads. Later, style and beauty were demanded, so the type has improved in appearance and size but retained the easy riding gaits.

The breed was developed from the Narragansett Pacers, the Canadian Pacers, the Morgans, and Thoroughbred breeds. There has always been some controversy about the origin of the two pacing breeds. Regardless of their origin, they were similar in appearance and gaits.

The Canadian Pacers were developed in Canada and brought into the United States.

The Narragansett Pacers were developed in Rhode Island. These two breeds contributed the mixed gaits from which the American Saddle Horse has derived his easy riding gaits. The Thoroughbred and Morgan contributed to the size, quality, and beauty of the breed.

The American Saddle Horse became extremely popular in American horse shows and is noted for beauty, style, high action, and ability to go either three or five gaits. These horses vary from 14.3 to 16.1 hands in height and from 900 to 1200 pounds in weight. Practically all of the solid colors are found, with the chestnut predominating. Excessive white markings about the face and legs are uncommon.

In the showing of the five-gaited saddle horse, the mane and tail are full, with the mane trained to fall on the right side. The foretop and first lock of mane are braided with ribbon. He wears quarter boots. The three-gaited saddle horse has his mane roached and his tail shaved a short way from

Below and opposite: The long tail, which is a distinctive feature of the breed, is evident in these two views of a striking black American Saddle Horse.

the base of the tail. He does not wear quarter boots or any artificial appliances. Both types of saddle horses usually have their tails set.

The Tennessee Walking Horse is one of the oldest recognized breeds in the United States, with most of the registered horses being descendants of the same recognized sires and dams. The history and pedigrees of some of the foundation stock reveal the fact that the breed is closely related to the Standardbred breed and the American Saddle Horse. Some of the ancestors were harness horses with good records in harness racing. Through the American Saddle Horse they were more remotely influenced by the Thoroughbred and Morgan. Many of the best ones trace to those early American Saddle Horses that carried a great amount of the breeding of the Narragansett and Canadian Pacers, and it is largely from this source that the running walk gait was inherited.

The gait is faster than the flat footed walk, with a speed of six to nine miles an hour. However, stress is placed on perfection of the gait rather than speed. In performance, the horse brings the front foot down just before the diagonal opposite hind foot. The hind foot over-steps the track of the front foot with a smooth, sliding motion from six

to fifteen inches. However, overstepping of the track of the front foot should not be carried to the extreme. The foot movements are accompanied by a nodding head, swinging ears and clicking teeth. The gait is pleasant to ride and is easy on the horse. Besides the running walk gait, the horse should have a good flat-footed walk with a speed of four to five miles an hour. The third gait is the canter. It is easy, graceful and comfortable to the rider.

Some strains of the Walking Horse have a tendency to break into the pacing gait when urged too much or when improperly managed. For this reason, those that are square gaited are preferred, as they are less likely to break their gait, since pacing horses are generally disliked by practical horsemen.

The Tennessee Walking Horse is easy to train, as the principle gait is a natural gait. The running walk can be improved and increased in speed by riding on a dirt road and urging the horse to greater speed but restraining him with the bit to keep him from breaking into a trot. The walk too is improved and increased by constant riding at this gait. It is natural for the horse to gallop, so the trainer has to restrain the natural gallop until it becomes a slow, easy 'rocking chair' canter.

Below: An American Saddlebred and owner. This breed is an excellent horse for riding.
Opposite: *This Tennessee Walking Horse, Coin's Hard Cash, was the 1987 Grand Champion.*

Instead of breeding for the style and flash of the American Saddle Horse, the breeders of Tennessee Walking Horses traditionally tended toward development of an easy gaited riding horse. The running walk was traditionally known as a plantation gait, as horses with an easy riding, running walk were used by plantation owners and overseers who spent long hours in the saddle. Tennessee Walking Horses were the favored mounts of rural doctors in the southeast in the late nineteenth century. Thus the breed was developed for utility, and not for show purposes. It is a tribute to the breed that they remained nearly pure in breeding for many years without the benefit of an organized registry.

When the breed Association was founded in 1935, pedigrees were accepted as remembered and recorded by the breeders. Until the 1940s, they were confined to the Southern United States, but are now found throughout North America and abroad.

The Tennessee Walking Horse averages 15.2 hands tall and weighs from 1000 to 1250 pounds. They have larger bones than the American Saddle Horse, while being short-backed, deep bodied and close coupled. The head is plainer and larger than the head of the American Saddle Horse, while resembling both that of the American Saddle Horse and the Standardbred. They have thin necks, set on well muscled and sloping shoulders. Some of them are more sloping in the croup and more curved in the hocks than other types of riding horses. They have large, flat cannons and dense bone. The feet are sound and of ample size. The coloration of Tennessee Walking Horses varies, and individuals may be sorrel, chestnut, black, bay, brown, gray, roan, yellow, or pure

Below: Tennessee Walking Horses at a competition. With their fine form and distinctive gait, they are a popular horse in equestrian events.
Opposite: A Tennessee Walking Horse stallion calmly regards the world from his stable south of Nashville.

white. The sorrels, chestnuts and yellows often have flaxen or white manes and tails.

The Tennessee Walking Horse is noted for its quiet, even-tempered disposition. Perhaps because of its disposition, it is a long-lived breed, frequently living for 25 to 30 years. Because of its size, temperament and gaits, the Walking Horse is a real general purpose horse. Many are used on rural farms, and the mares are frequently bred for mule production.

The Mangalarga of Brazil and the Criollo of Argentina are native breeds of horses that sprang from the original Spanish horses taken from Spain. Though many good polo ponies have been produced by crossing the Criollo and Thoroughbred, in the early twentieth century it was realized that the breed might be destroyed by crossing with Thoroughbred horses, and a group of interested horse breeders organized the Rural Argentine Society to preserve the purity of the Criollo horse. Criollos and Mangalargas, as well as the related Caballo of Chile, have been used for very long endurance rides in South America, and one 14-year-old horse is noted to have travelled 857 miles in seventeen days.

Below and opposite: The Peruvian Paso is a variation on the family of South American saddle horse breeds that includes the Criollo of Argentina and the Mangalarga of Brazil.

The Palomino, the beautiful, golden-colored stock horse of the western United States, emerged in the middle twentieth century as one of the most popular American breeds. Down through the ages there have been Palomino-colored horses and the color has always had its champions. Golden-colored horses are mentioned in ancient literature. However, they were not specifically bred as a type until the nineteenth century.

Golden-colored horses which evolved from the dun and buckskin horses brought by the Spanish to Mexico, Palominos were first bred in California and northern Mexico, but they are now being bred throughout North America and elsewhere. The exact origin of the Palomino cannot be definitely determined, as they were developed from a type and color that evolved without planning. After the type and color became evident, advocates began to breed horses with that in mind. This careful selection tended to cause Palomino colored horses to become excellent, well-bred stock horses. Mexican breeders have played a key role in developing the breed, and Mexico today produces many excellent Palomino horses.

There are two stories concerning the possible origin of the Palomino horse. One story states that in about 1800, Don Estaban, Mayor de Ganado or cattle foreman for the Mission at Santa Barbara, California, wanted to possess the finest saddle horse in the country. With this in mind, he offered a prize of brandy and money to anyone that would bring him such a horse. In the fall when the range mares and their colts were brought in from the range to act as threshing machines by tromping the wheat to separate the grain and straw, a mission worker discovered a cinnamon colored yearling with white mane

and tail. This yearling, when presented to Don Estaban, pleased him greatly. When the chaff was brushed off a beautiful golden coat was revealed. The colt, besides being beautiful in color, was gentle, graceful, and showed Arabian breeding.

An alternate story tells of a group of Native Americans who stole a fine white stallion near Altar, Sonora in northern Mexico. The next year they took a buckskin mare. The following summer, which was in about 1740, the mare returned with a golden-colored colt with white mane and tail. As the two dates are so far apart, perhaps there may be a relationship between the horses concerned in the stories. Very likely the two stories are apocryphal, but they do reflect a love and admiration for Palomino horses.

Right and opposite: The distinctive coloration of the Palomino makes it an extremely popular show breed. It is rare to see a show where Palominos are not present.

Certainly, the Spanish of California were very fond of good looking and useful riding horses and spent a great deal of money buying and breeding horses.

It was a custom among the Spanish Dons to give Palominos as gifts, to a friend or a favorite son. Otherwise these horses were kept for their owner's personal use and for their daughters' weddings. The Americans that settled in California and the Southwest were greatly influenced by the fashions of the Spanish and adopted many of their customs, including their preference for Palomino horses.

Besides breeding for the golden yellow color with white mane and tail, the stockmen bred for stamina and speed. So we find that they developed reasonable speed for stock horses, along with remarkable endurance. One story is recorded that General John C Fremont, following the American occupation of California in 1847, was at Los Angeles and wanted to go to Monterey and return. He borrowed two Canelos, the light-colored Palominos, and made the round trip of eight hundred miles in seven days.

The Palomino Horse Association and Stud Book Registry was officially formed in 1932 with noted Palomino researcher Dick Halliday as its executive secretary. Halliday had loved the Palomino color as a boy and never ceased his quest for knowledge of Palominos. While breeders of Palominos may differ with Halliday as to his opinions on breeding and registering horses, most appreciate his promotion work. The

Palomino Horse Breeders of America was formed in 1941 by breeders in California and Texas, and they publish the official Stud Book and Registry of Palominos.

Among some of the early Palomino horses there was evidently a dash of the draft breeds. This occurred when the buckskin and Palomino-colored mares were mated at random on the large western ranches. However, exceedingly few of the number with draft breeding were registered. The breeding of these few was generally unknown to the parties registering them. Some beautifully colored Palomino horses are occasionally found among the wild herds in the western states.

The various shades of yellow hair known as Palomino color may be on black, yellow or pink skin. The mane and tail in all cases should be pure white or ivory color. The preferred skin color is almost black. The pink skin is the skin without pigment, usually found underneath the white hair of pure white horses. The much discussed 'pumpkin-skin,' or yellow skin, is about the color of a bright yellow pumpkin. Ideally, a

Below: Albinos of the Pawnee Bill Wild West Show, headquartered near Pawnee, Oklahoma.
Opposite: Horses of the Albino breed are not technically albinos, as they have normal pigmentation. Rather, they are bred to have a pure white overall coat.

Palomino is said to be the color of a 'newly-minted gold coin.' Some breeders prefer horses having white markings on the legs and white on their face, while others prefer their horses to have dark legs with some white in the face. The Palomino has many uses and use will vary almost as much as the breeds from which they derive most of their breeding. A few of the Palomino colored Quarter Horses are extensively used in stock work. Many are used as dude and trail horses where beauty and a safe, slow, comfortable ride is desired. Because of their attractive appearance many are used as trick and parade horses.

The Albino Horse, like the Palomino, is a breed of mixed heritage that is bred for specific coloration. Not literally albino, the breed is simply an all-white variation on the Morgan Horse type. An albino is actually an animal suffering from a congenital lack of pigmentation and having white hair, white skin and pink eyes. As a breed, Albinos have a white coat, but natural pigmentation. If the color was recessive the pure whites would produce only pure whites when mated

together, but very few pure whites when mated with horses of another color. A white horse among a wild band is very rare, but a few have been seen.

The Albino breed originated in Nebraska in 1918, when CR and HB Thompson of Swan Lake, Nebraska, purchased a pure white stallion named Old King from Professor William Newell of Illinois. Old King had sired many snow white colts in Illinois and many of them were used as circus horses. Old King was mated with Morgan mares and 50 per cent of the colts were born pure white.

In 1924, the Thompsons moved to Stuart, Nebraska. At Stuart, they purchased some cream colored, yellow skinned mares, the descendants of a local yellow colored stallion named Yellow Cat. These mares, when mated to white stallions, produced about 50 per cent white colts, 25 per cent cream colored colts with white manes and tails and 25 per cent golden colored colts with black manes and tails. Yellow Cat was said to have been born in an area of Missouri famous for Quarter Horses.

The Yellow Cat mares carried some Spanish breeding. Yellow Cat, too, weighed about 1200 pounds and was 15.2 hands tall.

Some line breeding was done. The whites of the first, second, and third generations were mated together. The percentage of pure white colts has increased until the colts of the fourth generation are almost all white.

Other white horses were developed simultaneously, but apart from the group at Stuart, Nebraska. Sometimes their breeding has been unknown, but one large herd of white horses in Wyoming started from a pure white stallion purchased in Illinois. His sire was used in the Ringling Brothers' Circus and was possibly related to Old King. This band was later developed by crossing with Morgan mares, much the same as those at White Horse Place of Stuart, Nebraska. Some of the first cross white mares are now being mated to Thoroughbred stallions. In 1937, a group of horse breeders started the American Albino Horse Club to preserve and promote the breeding of their pure white, pink skinned horses.

The Albino is born pure white. The skin is pink and should not be specked with pigment. As a rule the eyes are dark, but a few have glassy blue eyes. The hoofs are from white to a slight cream color.

The Albinos have clean cut, wide, straight, well proportioned heads with short ears. The neck is medium long and well carried. They have a heavy mane and tail. Other conformation characteristics are a wide chest, a great spring of ribs, a short back and level croup. The shoulders and withers blend smoothly with the body. The withers are well defined but not high and sharp. They are deep in front and rear flank. They have medium bones, straight legs and clean joints. Their feet are well shaped and of superior quality. The density and hardness of the hoof will convince anyone of the fallacy of the old statement that 'white hoofs are soft.' They are from 14.2 to 16 hands tall and weigh from 1000 to 1200 pounds. In type they are one of the most uniform of the recently promoted color breeds.

The conformation and set of feet and legs cause the Albinos to be good travellers. They have endurance, durability and medium speed. As a whole the gaits are the walk, trot and canter. However, a few of the Wyoming strain do a good running walk. Albinos are even-tempered, yet active. They are smart and easily trained.

Below: The Albino, like the Palomino and Appaloosa, is bred not for conformation or utility, but because of distinctive coloration.

Opposite: The Appaloosa originated in the mountains of eastern Oregon and the Idaho Panhandle, and was first bred by the Nez Perce Native Americans.

Like the Albino and the Palomino, the Appaloosa is a type descended from the early Spanish horses that is bred for its distinctive coloration. The Appaloosa is said to have been developed by the Nez Perce Native Americans of the Palouse country of central Idaho and eastern Washington, although it is doubtful if all horses of this peculiar color had their origin among the horses owned by the Nez Perce.

These Native Americans were splendid horsemen, and developed the Appaloosa for war horses. They bred for the peculiar color markings and for sturdy riding horses. After the Nez Perce were placed on reservations in 1877, some of the horses were appropriated by others and the breeding stock was widely scattered. Many Appaloosa horses were left in Montana and helped to spread this type throughout the Rocky Mountain states.

Some horses were taken from the Nez Perce Native American Reservation of Idaho to the Pine Ridge Native American Reservation in South Dakota in 1893. Peter Shangrear, who took these horses to the Pine Ridge Reservation, described them as being roan with red spots, bay with white spots, and black with white spots. All of them had white over their hips with round spots of other color. They had a white ring around the

Below: This young Appaloosa foal displays his breed's characteristic coloration.

Opposite: An Appaloosa mare prowls her corral.

dark of the eye. Many of them had a light mane and tail. Shangrear sold the stallions and geldings but bred the mares.

In 1938, the Appaloosa Horse Club was formed at Moro, Oregon, for the registering of Appaloosas. As a type, they are usually closely coupled, short-backed and clean-legged horses with good feet. Their sturdy conformation appeals to the stockmen and many are used as stock horses. Their flashy markings appeal to the eastern people, who often think a western horse should be some unusual color. The Appaloosa horses are very prepotent and readily stamp their pattern upon their colts out of plain colored mares. The color is widely distributed. It is sometimes found in the wild horse bands, especially the red roan Appaloosa color. While the color has generally been restricted to horses of stock horse type occasionally a horse of light draft size has Appaloosa markings. The color is inherited from the smaller horses, and some of the Spanish ponies of South Texas are of this color.

Spotted horses are horses of two colors, one always being white. In the United States, such horses are generally known as either Paints or Pintos, with the latter appellation being more common in the West. In September 1941, when an association was started to register horses of this broken color pattern, it was named the Pinto Horse Society, and in 1963, the American Paint Horse Association was formed.

The Pinto color is bred because it is pleasing to the eye, and not because of utility. The color was traditionally popular with Native Americans, and some tribes developed large horses of striking appearance. Pintos were, in fact, once referred to as 'Indian ponies.'

There are two basic Paint or Pinto patterns. The piebald color pattern is black and white, while skewbald is a color pattern of white and some color other than black. Horses of white and cream color are called Palomino-Pintadas by the Palomino Horse Association. The color pattern has been passed down from early Spanish horses having some Shetland pony breeding. If the Pinto Horses are called a breed and have certain standards of size, conformation, color, and action by which they are judged the breed will improve and become more uniform in type, color and breed character.

The Pinto Horse Society has drawn their descriptive terms from Argentina, where the

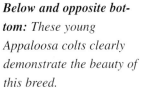

Below and opposite bottom: *These young Appaloosa colts clearly demonstrate the beauty of this breed.*
Opposite top: *This Paint colt subtly displays the characteristics of his breed's coloration.*

Pinto markings are divided into two groups, Overo and Tobiano. In the Overo pattern the white spots start at the belly and extend upward; the back, mane and tail are dark. The face is often white and the eyes are blue or the color known as 'glass eyes.' The pattern is often very irregular. In the Tobiano pattern, the white starts at the back and extends downward. The spots are larger and more regular in shape. These animals are not 'glass eyed' as often as the Overo colored horses. They are more likely to have dark colored heads, but the feet and legs are often white. The differences in the pattern are difficult to describe but not difficult to recognize when one examines a few pictures or sees a few horses of the proper pattern. In type Pintos fit into the description for a sturdy type of stock horse. They have short, strong backs, are well proportioned, and their parts blend together smoothly.

In the early twentieth century, a few people called Pinto Horses 'Arabians.' This was the result of circus terminology, in which circus horses of white and spotted colors were often called Arabians as it added to the glamour of the show. All purebred Arabians imported into or bred in the

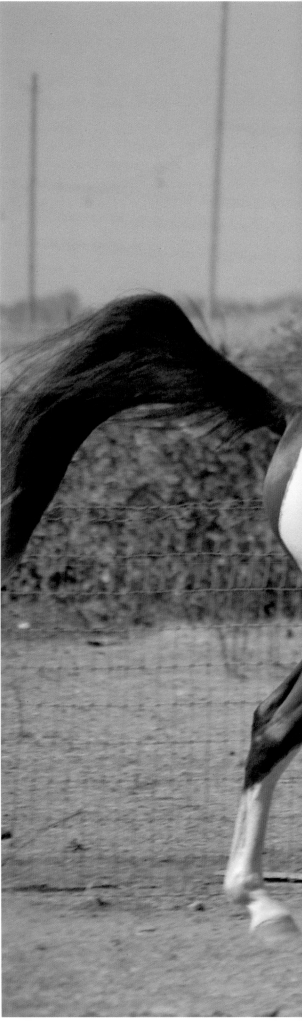

United States have been of some solid color.

Some Pintos have Shetland blood and are smaller than other horses. Those that do not have Shetland blood will average in size with the other light riding types of the West. Some Pintos have been mated for several generations with purebred stallions and have produced spirited horses with excellent conformation. The fact that many Pintos have won in shows where all types of stock horses compete is evidence of their good conformation. Those with more than half white are the most attractive. A strip in the face, a star or a snip on the nose are favored over bald faces. Some white in the mane and tail is attractive but not often found. Glass eyes are not liked as well as the normal eye color, but they will occur part of the time with this color pattern.

The Colorado Ranger horses were horses developed in the early twentieth century by stockmen who had the stock-working qualities of their horses in mind. The stallions were generally bred under range conditions and the colts developed on the range. Sturdy stock horses varying in size, they were noted for leopard markings on a white skin. When such are crossed with other light horses, the coat color is often an Appaloosa color, though some were solid in color, some pure white, and some of a Palomino color.

Below: A Pinto mare with a touch of white on her neck.

Opposite: This playful young Pinto carries the highly contrasting colors that are archetypical of the breed.

Overleaf: The patterns that occur in Pintos are interesting and widely varied.

TROTTING AND HARNESS BREEDS

Below and opposite: The Cleveland Bay is the archetypical British royal coach horse. In the picture below HM Queen Elizabeth II inspects her Palace Horse Guards.

The Cleveland Bay is the oldest existing general purpose breed of horses. These sturdy horses originated as carriage horses in the Cleveland district of Yorkshire, England. The breed developed from the earlier English breed called the Northumberland Chapman Horse. Before the roads were improved for wagon or carriage traffic, the Chapman horses had been used to pack loads of merchandise. Thoroughbred blood was introduced to give refinement and improve the type.

The Cleveland Bay resembles a large, well developed Thoroughbred but has more bone and muscle. The heart girth is 80 inches or better and the cannon bone measures nine to 10 inches. Cleveland Bays have been criticized for long backs, but by careful selection this fault has been overcome to a great extent. They are 16 to 17 hands tall and

weigh 1250 to 1550 pounds and are an active, fast walking breed that stand the summer heat well. The color is always bay with black mane and tail. White markings are almost unknown.

Soon after 1800 Cleveland Bay horses were imported to the United States. Some were used for the carriage and farm trade and some were crossed with Thoroughbreds to produce hunters. After the advent of the automobile, interest in the breed dropped off until the mid twentieth century. At that time imported English horses were used for crossing with Thoroughbreds for the production of hunters. It has been said that the better hunters are produced from mating Thoroughbred mares with Cleveland stallions than are produced by the reverse cross. This claim has also been made in England, where more extensive crossing has been done.

Traditionally, stallions were crossed with draft mares to produce a medium type of horse for farm purposes. Cleveland horses were seen as serving a very useful purpose, both as a pure breed or for crossing. They were sufficiently large to meet the demand of most farmers who favored medium sized farm horses. It will be some time before purebreds will be plentiful enough to be used to any great extent for general work.

The Cleveland Bay also influenced many American horses up to the beginning of the twentieth century, when the need for carriage horses began to wane. They were used in the earlier days as carriage and wagon horses and were crossed with the native mares of the West. Such crosses were also useful as saddle horses. The grade descendants of these earlier Cleveland sires continued to influence the range bands, but by the 1940s, their identity had been lost through many crosses with other breeds and types.

Having originated in the same part of England, the Yorkshire Coach Horse was very similar to the Cleveland Bay and was also used as a carriage horse. The breed was also influenced by the Northumberland Chapman Horses, which were used as wagon or carriage horses. Like the Cleveland Bay, the Yorkshire Coach Horses were imported to the United States to be used for carriage and farm animals. Also like the Cleveland horses, they were seen as serving a very useful purpose, both as a pure breed or for crossing, and were sufficiently large to meet the demand of most farmers who favored medium sized horses.

The Morgan breed developed in Vermont from a very prepotent stallion named Justin Morgan after his owner. There are many

Below: These Morgan trotters are practicing for a demonstration to be given at the San Francisco Horse Show. Opposite: A portrait of a handsome Morgan stallion.

conflicting stories as to his breeding. It has been said that his breeding was Arabian, Thoroughbred, Canadian and Dutch. A generally accepted story is that he was related to the Thorough-bred, although he was born about 1789, before the Thoroughbred had developed into a definite type.

Justin Morgan lived under adverse conditions. His owners did not always prize him as they should have since he changed hands several times to satisfy a debt. In spite of adverse conditions he sired many good colts and stamped his characteristics upon his descendants for several generations. Justin Morgan was described as 'the big little horse,' both because of his conformation and ability. He seems to have been the ideal general purpose horse, for the popular expression was that he could out-draw, out-walk, out-trot and out-run every horse that was ever matched against him. He is described as a small, dark bay. His body was round with a great spring of ribs. He was short-backed and deep bodied. In action he was active and proud. He was a very hardy stallion and was sound and in good health when

Below: Coloration can vary widely from mare to foal.
Opposite: A frisky Morgan colt at play.

he received an injury that caused his death at the age of 32 years. By the time that the profound merit of this amazing horse was fully appreciated, he was dead and the breed then developed by concentrating the blood of his descendants.

The Morgan has contributed to the breeding that developed both the American Saddle Horse and the Standardbred. The Morgan usually is closely coupled, strong-backed, medium in length of neck, and fairly deep and wide, with a level croup. Their height varies from 14.2 to 15.2 hands, and they usually weigh about 1000 pounds. Some Morgans are low and round over the withers. They have excellent quality of bone and good feet. Bay seems to be the prevailing color, followed by chestnut, brown, and black.Today some Morgan breeding is found in the pedigrees of most of the color types,

Below and opposite: As can be seen with these Morgan colts, the coloration of the members of this breed can vary widely, from chestnut to black.

such as the Palomino, and Morgan breeding may be found in a few Quarter Horses.

In 1907, Colonel Joseph Battel donated a tract of land in Middlebury, Vermont to the United States Government to be used as a Morgan breeding farm. General Gates, a black Morgan stallion born in 1894, was selected to head the stud. Horses bred at this farm have done a great deal to perpetuate the type of Morgans, as descendants of General Gates now head several studs throughout the nation, including the one at Point Reyes National Seashore in Northern California.

The Morgan horses have also been very important in developing the western horse of the early days. While there were not many purebred Morgan breeders in the West, many stockmen bought good Morgan stallions in the East and took them West to 'grade up' the light horses. Some people carried on the grading process for several years, and by the middle of the twentieth century, certain range bands show a great deal of Morgan blood.

The earlier Morgans were close coupled and somewhat deeper and blockier than the present day eastern Morgan horse. They were in great demand for cow ponies, and in the earlier days were sometimes used for polo ponies. Many Morgans were also crossed with Thoroughbreds and produce excellent stock for use as cow horses and pleasure horses, as well as light work horses.

Purebred Morgans are still used by a few ranchers, and groups of Morgan horses may be found in a purer state than the Standardbreds. California, Montana, Illinois and Texas are among the leading states in the breeding of Morgan horses. White markings are not found to any considerable extent. The Morgan is often very fast for a short distance, and sometimes makes a creditable showing in quarter-mile races. Morgans also have an excellent reputation in endurance rides.

The German Coach Horses were the largest of the coach breed and more nearly approached the draft horses in size. They too were used to some extent in the West, but their influence was not of much importance. The Hackney is the most modern carriage horse. Animals of this breed are used almost exclusively for show purposes in the United States.

THE STANDARDBRED

Below: A Standardbred in harness struts his stuff.
Opposite: While they are a joy to watch at horse shows, Standardbreds are also a beauty to behold.

The Standardbred is a breed of trotters and pacers developed in the United States. The breed started in New York and the New England states and was derived from the Thoroughbred, Norfolk Trotters, Narragansett Pacers, Canadian Pacers, Arabians, and Morgans. The breed generally traces its heritage to the oriental sires that helped develop the Thoroughbred. The reason for the development of the Standardbred was economics. During the horse and buggy days of the late nineteenth and early twentieth centuries, before good roads and the automobile, many Standardbred or roadster horses were used. A good team was a pleasure to its owner, so large sums of money were sometimes spent to secure the very best driving horses. Standardbreds are not as large as Thoroughbreds, but their long forearms and muscles enable them to extend to great speeds while trotting or pacing. They have influenced the nature of harness racing all over Europe, as well as in Russia, Australia and New Zealand.

Hambletonian, the great sire of the Standardbred, was by Abdallah, by Mambrino, by Messenger. Messenger was a gray Thoroughbred imported to the United States in 1786 who traces his heritage to Darley Arabian. Messenger's descendants had the ability to trot and were bred for trotting ability. As Hambletonian is the most

84

important family of the Standardbred, all horses of Standardbred breeding have been referred to as 'Hambletonians.'

The Norfolk Trotters came from England and were the ancestors of the present Hackney breed. The Norfolk Trotters, combined with the blood of Messenger, contributed to the trotting gait. The Morgan breed had been established before the Standardbred, and many of the early harness race horses carried Morgan breeding. The Hambletonian trotters were generally faster than the Morgan, and the Morgan influence became less important.

The Narragansett Pacers were a Colonial type found in the New England states and Virginia that descended from Spanish Jennets, which were, in turn, descendants of Arabian and Barb horses taken to Spain by the Moors several centuries earlier. Other references indicate that they were related to the Ambling horses that existed in England before the development of the Thoroughbred. The Narragansett Pacers were later absorbed by other breeds. Likewise, there are conflicting opinions as to the gait of the Spanish Jennet, but evidence indicates that they were probably pacers. At any rate it is known that the Narragansett Pacers and Canadian Pacers were crossed with other light driving and riding horses and contributed to the pacing gait of the Standardbred breed and to the saddle gaits of the American Saddle Horse. The Standardbred horses have influenced the light western horse as much or more than any other breed. Today a few range horses show almost enough trotting or pacing conformation to pass as pure Standardbred horses.

Brief descriptions of Canadian Pacers show them to be a more rugged horse than the Narragansett Pacers. The source of the two breeds was evidently about the same.

While the Standardbred originated in New York and New England, they were taken to Kentucky and Tennessee and contributed to the American Saddle Horse and the Tennessee Walking Horse. The rich bone building soil of the two states caused many fast driving horses to be developed in that region, and today Kentucky leads in producing the fastest Standardbred horses. On the whole, the breed has developed and been maintained in the Atlantic and Midwestern states where harness racing is popular. The Standardbred horse is a light harness type and is remarkably fast at the trot or pace.

It is said that the Standardbred horse is born with an inherent ability to trot or pace, and his racing career is generally determined by his natural preference. While the gaits of Standardbred horses can't be predicted with accuracy, some families show a

Opposite: Created specifically for trotting, the Standardbred is a beautiful animal. Standardbreds are not as large as Thoroughbreds, but their long forearms and muscles enable them to extend to great speeds while trotting or pacing. They have influenced the nature of harness racing throughout the world.

tendency to produce trotters and some to produce pacers.

Trotting and pacing for the best two out of three heats of a mile each caused the Standardbred to be developed for endurance, a characteristic which makes them useful for other work besides racing.

Standardbred horses are closely related to the American Saddle Horse, being developed from almost the same original stock. It is not unusual to find Standardbred horses that perform well under saddle, and some of them will do all the gaits desired of a five gaited saddle horse, so some are used as pleasure saddle horses and some are developed into good stock horses. Range mares of the Standardbred type, when crossed with Thoroughbred stallions, produce excellent offspring, and these colts develop into a very good type of riding horse.

PONIES

Many of the important Pony breeds, such as the Shetland, the Dales and the Welsh, originated in Britain. These small horses are distinct from other breeds for their having been isolated from other stock since the Bronze Age and having developed independently — as the Shetland Pony did in the Shetland Islands off Scotland. The Shetland Islands are rough, the soil poor, and vegetation scant. In these adverse conditions the Shetland does not develop much size.

Standing only 10 hands or less, the Shetland is the smallest of the Ponies. Bred primarily as a riding horse for children, Shetlands became popular in the nineteenth century, and were imported into North America. In type the native Pony resembles a miniature draft horse, but in the United States selection is often made for trimness, and the type and quality of a true saddle horse. In color individuals may be solid or 'spotted.' The 'spotted' Ponies usually have dark heads. The solid colors are mostly mouse brown and black. The 'spotted' Ponies may have 'glass' eyes. This color has a popular appeal but may be objected to in showing.

When the crossing has been with Thoroughbreds the Ponies have often been very fast, and one Thoroughbred-Shetland Pony developed into a very fast calf-roping Pony.

As the name suggests, the Welsh Pony originated in the mountains of Wales. Slightly larger than the Shetland, the Welsh

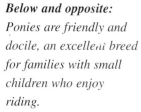

Below and opposite:
Ponies are friendly and docile, an excellent breed for families with small children who enjoy riding.

Pony stands 12 hands or less, though the Welsh Cob variant may stand up to 15 hands. The exact origin of the Welsh Pony is not known, but it is suspected that they descended from a prehistoric Pony type that was influenced by Arabian blood in Medieval times. In the 1940s, the breed almost vanished, but has subsequently been brought back from the edge of extinction. Welsh Ponies are very active and make excellent Ponies for older children. In Wales they were traditionally used to carry or pull grown people over the rough lands.

Unlike the Shetland, the Welsh Pony was not bred extensively in the United States, although other breeds of Ponies have been introduced from time to time.

The Icelandic Pony, like the Shetland, is an ancient breed, brought to Iceland when the Norse settled there in 874 AD. No other horses or ponies have been imported into Iceland for at least 800 years, so these may have the purest bloodlines of all the horses. These dun colored Ponies average 12 to 13 hands high.

In the extreme southern part of Texas along the Gulf of Mexico there were many small Ponies that are doubtless very pure in Spanish breeding. These Ponies are of various colors, but mostly of conservative colors

Below: *A handsome, almost Palomino-colored, Welsh Pony.*

Opposite: *The Icelandic Pony, like the Shetland, is descended from stock that developed in an isolated location, and hence is much smaller than Ponies such as the Welsh breed that has had contact with larger horses.*

of bay, brown, sorrel, and gray. Occasionally some buckskin and various shades of dun and cream colors may be found. Some may show the typical Appaloosa color markings over their hips. These Ponies are small, due to heredity, inbreeding, and partly because the grass upon which they develop is not very nutritious and is deficient in bone building material. Traditionally these Ponies were developed into fair riding Ponies that will weigh from one to two hundred pounds more than those left to develop on the native range. They will also gain two or three inches in height. Not many of these Ponies exceed 14.2 hands in height and 850 pounds in weight. They are short backed, clean legged, light boned in type, and are very hardy. They have been used extensively by ranchers for cow ponies because they have great endurance and weight packing ability.

The Pony of the Americas was developed from an Appaloosa mare and a Shetland stallion as a children's pony. The breed was established in the United States and Canada in 1956. Versatile and well balanced, the spotted Pony is an excellent trotting and jumping horse and is often used in competions for young riders. It stands 11.2 to 13 hands high.

Below: A group of New Forest ponies in Hampshire, England.
Opposite: The Pony of the Americas is a relatively new bred, created by a cross between Shetland Ponies and full-size Appaloosas. The Appaloosa heritage is obvious in this example. They are used in trotting and jumping competitions.

DRAFT HORSES

Below: A close-up view of the strong faces of a pair of Percherons.
Opposite: A Clydesdale team.

Distinct draft horse breeds exist in nearly every part of Europe. They are descended from the great war horses that were bred during the Middle Ages to carry heavily armored knights into battle, and have been developed over the intervening centuries as heavy duty work horses. Though they were superseded in many of their traditional tasks by trucks after the second decade of the twentieth century, draft horses are still seen even today in rural parts of England, France and Germany, and especially in Eastern Europe.

There are also still many high-grade draft horses in North America, although they are less common than in Europe. In North America, the breeds are mixed, but the Percheron and Belgian have traditionally ex-

ceeded the other draft breeds in numbers. The latter were typically more popular among the smaller ranchers, while the Percheron was considered by many to be better on the large ranges. The claim has been made that the Percheron is more active, gets a greater colt crop, and lives better under range conditions.

Some of the best Percheron and Belgian horses in the United States were traditionally found in the Pacific Coast states. The grade draft horses of the West generally have better wind, denser bone, sounder hoofs, and possess greater endurance than horses produced in the East. Being raised in the open, they are very healthy and spirited. They have a great reputation for being exceedingly willing work horses and are well liked by farmers in the farming states when they are trained to work. Some are shipped without training and the farmers that are accustomed to gentle horses are afraid of them and buy them at too great a discount.

Under range conditions, the grade draft horses do not attain the growth that they do in the farming environment where they would receive better care and feed. Not many draft horses are produced on the range that will exceed 1400 pounds. However,

Below: A tender moment between a Clydesdale stallion and mare. Having originated in Scotland, Clydesdales are now popular in America.

some that are cared for on farms may exceed this weight. Occasionally light horses are used as work horses, but most work horses carry some draft breeding. Some of the range horses having one-fourth or more draft breeding may be used for riding horses. Originally this was thought desirable because of the increased size and substance, but their sluggish disposition, slow speed, and clumsy action have checked their use for this purpose. Some are still used on dude ranches for pack horses and some may be used for riding.

England is home to the Shire Horse, which is descended from the war horses of the Middle Ages. The Old English Heavy Horse, also known as the Great Horse or Black Horse, was the largest ever known breed of horse,

standing 19 or 20 hands and weighing over 3000 pounds. Shire Horses are still very large, standing 17.3 hands and weighing up to a ton.

After the change in type of warfare, the Shire evolved from a war horse into an agricultural and commercial horse. Such animals were used as cart horses for pulling huge carts about city streets. When an Association was formed in 1878 it was called 'The English Cart Horse Society,' although in 1884 the name was changed to the Shire Horse Society.

The Shire is more upstanding than the Belgian but about the same in weight. Individuals are massive, wide, and deep. They are active, long-lived, and good breeders. They are a proud and powerful creature that can pull a skid with up to twice their own weight. They have longer bodies than most of the other draft breeds. A heavy, flat bone is characteristic of the breed, and they have an abundance of long hair growing from the back of the cannon. This long hair is called 'feather,' and the fineness of the

Below: A classic view of a great Shire Horse. A descendant of the war horses of Medieval England, they are Britain's archetypical draft breed. Note the feathering about the ankles that is typical of draft breeds.

feather is an indication of quality. Some people claim the presence of feather is one reason why the Shire has not been more popular in the United States.

Usually bay in color, the Shire may also be brown, black, chestnut, gray or even roan. Most Shires have some white on the legs and a streak or blaze on the face, but they are not as extensively marked as the Clydesdale.

The Shire has been criticized for roughness, steep pasterns and lack of quality in the feet, but the longer leg and body enable them to have a good, long, straight stride. The size of bone and feather is an asset when they are used for crossing with the light range mares of the West.

Shires are third in popularity in the United States. They have never been a show breed as have the Clydesdales. They have been used a great deal for grading up draft horses and have produced some excellent grade geldings.

A Scottish breed, the Clydesdale is the show breed of the draft horses. They are noted for quality, straight and high action,

and are used more often in six-horse and eight-horse teams of draft horses than any other breed. For example, the Anheuser Busch Brewing Company operates three demonstration teams of 18-hand Clydesdales in St Louis, Missouri; Merrimac, New Hampshire; and Romoland, California, which pull brewery wagons in parades.

Clydesdales look a great deal like Shires, being similar in color, except possibly more marked by white points than the Shire. They also have an abundance of feather. However, Clydesdales are very fine in quality, considering their size. They are noted for their sloping pasterns, good feet, and superior action. Many horse team drivers consider the Clydesdale to be the soundest of the draft breeds.

Clydesdale stallions weigh 1900 pounds or more, and the mares 1700 pounds, and both are quite tall, typically averaging between 16 and 17 hands.

Indigenous to Suffolk in England, the Suffolk breed dates to the beginning of the sixteenth century. These powerful and well-proportioned horses stand 16.2 hands and

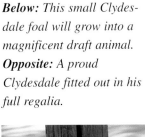

Below: This small Clydesdale foal will grow into a magnificent draft animal.
Opposite: *A proud Clydesdale fitted out in his full regalia.*

are typically a shade of chestnut. Color is recessive, and when Suffolks are mated together, the foals are always chestnut. White is found as a star, snip or small blaze, and on the hind ankles. In type, the Suffolk's head is rather long, bold and bony, with small ears. The neck is short, thick and arched. The body is rather long and round and there is a rounded smoothness throughout. Suffolks are a well muscled breed, showing good quality. The feet are round, of good size, and the bone has excellent texture. The action is straight and true, but not high.

The breed is noted for long life and the mares are very prolific. Some show stallions have weighed as much as 2300 pounds, but breeders prefer stallions from 1800 to 1900 pounds and mares from 1600 to 1650 pounds.

The Percheron originated in La Perche, Normandy in northwestern France. Previous to 1822 this breed was called Norman, and some horsemen in the United States called them 'Norman' horses instead of Percherons.

The Perche district is very strict on requirements, with a high standard that traditionally made it a superior horse region, and which is responsible for the development of this excellent breed.

Before the advent of railroads in France, the Percheron was used for pulling coaches and heavy wagons over dirt roads.

While some may be brown or chestnut, the Percheron is usually black and gray. In type the Percheron is deep, short, heavy muscled, and big boned. Individuals are short to medium in length of leg, the short

Below: *A magnificent Clydesdale.*
Opposite: *Draft horses, such as this handsome team of Belgians in field harness, still put in a day's work on farms.*

legged animals being preferred. Some individuals are shallow in body, steep in the croup, short and straight on the pasterns and travel wide. In size the stallions in show condition usually weigh over a ton and the mares 1800 to 2000 pounds. For work horses a smaller size is favored.

The Percheron was the first draft breed to be imported into North America, and it eventually became one of the most common such steeds on this continent. Today representatives of this breed are the most numerous draft breed in the United States and Canada, numbering over 250,000. They are also the most widely distributed of the draft breeds.

The Belgian breed evolved from the Flemish Horse, a large, coarse, black breed native to northern Europe in and around Flanders, which now straddles the border between France and Belgium. The Flemish horse was crossed with other breeds and carefully selected, and the result is the large, smooth turned breed we know today. The first Belgians were imported into North America in 1866, and a Breed Association was formed the same year by JD Conner, who remained as secretary for over 50 years. The Belgians are deep, wide and heavy muscled, with a great deal of substance. Stallions and mares in show condition have weighed well over a ton and 1800 pounds, respectively. Today smaller animals are preferred. Individuals are sometimes faulted for coarseness, low backs, and meaty hocks. The efforts of the Belgian breeders in the United States were traditionally to increase quality, set of feet and legs, and action.

The early Belgians were mostly bay in color, although today, Belgians may occur as sorrel, chestnut, or roan. The breed has traditionally had a strong tendency toward manes and tails of a lighter shade than their body color, many chestnuts having flaxen manes and tails.

In North America, western ranchers typically used many registered and grade Belgian stallions, and the breed had a marked influence on the farm and range horses in the early twentieth century. On the open range, they developed into 1300 to 1500 pound horses which were ideal for the farm trade.

Below: This team of coalblack Clydesdales is a stunning sight.
Opposite: A hard-working draft team in harness with a calliope.

HORSE RACING

Known as 'the Sport of Kings,' horse racing existed as an organized event in Egypt and the Middle East, and Homer even describes a horse race in his book *The Iliad* (xxiii). By the late middle ages, Newmarket in England was hosting regular, organized races. Horse racing is known to date from 1540 on the Roodee at Chester in England, but the first king known to enjoy 'the Sport of Kings' on a regular basis was James I of England (1566-1625), who attended races at Newmarket as early as 1605.

Today, the most important races in most countries are thought of in terms of a 'triple crown,' a group of three races, the winning of which is extremely prestigious, not to mention very lucrative. The three races are usually the three most important races to be run in a nation's racing season, and any horse able to win all three in a single year is accorded superstar status. The premier racing event in England is the British Triple Crown, which consists of the straight mile at Newmarket, run during the first week of May, the 2641-yard Derby at Epsom, run on the first Wednesday in June, and the mile and three-quarters, run at Doncaster in September. The entire British Triple Crown was first won by West Australian in 1853, and his feat has been equaled by only 14 colts since then. These are: Gladiateur (1865), Lord Jim (1866), Ormonde (1886), Common (1891), Isinglass (1893), Galtee More (1897), Flying Fox (1899), Diamond Jubilee (1900), Rock Sand (1903), Pommern

(1915), Gay Crusader (1917), Gainsborough (1918) and Bahram (1935).

In England, there is no horse race more important than the Derby, the race from which the Kentucky race takes its name. The Derby itself takes its name from the Earl of Derby, who first sponsored the race in 1780. Like the newer race at Churchill Downs, the Derby is open to three-year-olds. The course was intended to be one mile and a half (2640 yards), but instead is 2641 yards due to a survey error. Except for six years during World War II, when the race was held at Newmarket, the Derby has been held annually on the first Wednesday of June at Epsom Downs near London.

Other important English races are the two mile and a quarter Ascot Gold Cup, inaugurated in 1807, the two and a half mile Goodwood Cup, organized in 1812, and the two mile, five furlong Doncaster Cup, which dates from 1766, making it perhaps the oldest major race in the world.

In Ireland, where horse racing is an extremely important part of the national sporting life, there is a Triple Crown consist-

ing of the Irish 200 Guineas (1921), the Irish Derby (1866) and the Irish St Leger (1915), which are a mile, a mile and a half and a mile and three-quarters, respectively.

In the North America, racing came with the first horses, as the Spaniards had some stock described as suitable for racing. Organized racing developed first in Virginia and the Carolinas during the reign of George II (1727-1760), and has remained important in these areas ever since. George Washington, one of Virginia's pre-eminent citizens, was also a well-known horse breeder. Kentucky had become an important breeding center by 1795, and in the north, important races were first held on Long Island in 1819. The English had a track laid out in the locality of the present Belmont Park. It has been a leading section ever since.

In the Southern colonies, conditions favored short, fast races so quarter-mile racing was developed. The sport became the popular sport of the colonies before the Revolution. The Revolutionary War and the War of 1812 retarded racing. The Civil War almost stopped racing entirely and caused

Below: Thoroughbreds on display at Ireland's Curragh racetrack.
Opposite bottom: A race horse in training.
Opposite top: Racing at Newmarket in Suffolk, one of England's greatest courses.

the abandonment of some of the best Thoroughbred breeding farms, especially in the South. Since that time, due to the fact there have been no wars waged on this continent, racing has not suffered to such a marked extent.

The early races were generally in the four mile class, but by 1880, those of distances less than two miles became the rule. From the turn of the century until 1920 — in part because of the grueling four-mile races — racing was made illegal in all American states except Maryland and Kentucky. The latter was in deference to the fact that the most important American race takes place in May at Churchill Downs in Louisville, Kentucky. The Kentucky Derby, with its multimillion dollar purse, is the most important race in America, and perhaps the world.

The fastest time for this mile and a quarter race was 1:59.4, run by Secretariat, who went on to win the entire Triple Crown in 1973. In so doing, Secretariat beat the time of Northern Dancer, who had set a record of two minutes flat in 1964. No horse has come close to Secretariat's time since, although in 1993, Sea Hero won a purse of $735,900, which was a record in its own right, and nearly five times what Secretariat earned two decades earlier.

In the twentieth century, racing evolved into a popular sport, both from the standpoint of the horse owners and the race-going public. The early races were generally matched races, whereas now the races are for a number of horses. Except for the short sprint races, most of the races were long endurance contests of three heats of four miles each. Two-year-old racing, not known in the early days, became popular. Betting that was of a private nature has changed until it is a well-organized business. The parimutuel system popularized betting.

The history of racing and the development of the Thoroughbred horse is closely related to legislation concerning racing. Adverse legislation took Tennessee from among the top states in Thoroughbred breeding, but positive legislation turned that around. After 1920, the return of racing to California stimulated Thoroughbred breeding in that state. Breeding of other classes of livestock has likewise been stimulated as a result of the support racing has been given at state fairs.

Racing and Thoroughbred breeding has gone hand in hand. In 1942, there were 6400 registered Thoroughbreds in the United States, and half a century later, there were half a million. Purses have increased in amount and number. Sea Hero, who in 1993 won almost five times as much money as Secretariat in 1973, won 12 times as much as was won by the great Whirlaway in 1941.

Today, the American Triple Crown consists of three individual races, which are, themselves, three of the most important single races in America. These are the Kentucky Derby (first run in 1875), the Preakness Stakes (first run in 1876) and the Belmont Stakes (first run in 1869). They are open to three-year-old colts, geldings or fillies and are a mile and a quarter, a mile and three-sixteenths, and a mile and a half in length, respectively. Since it was first accomplished in 1919, only eleven horses have won all three races of the American Triple Crown. They are Sir Barton (1919), Gallant Fox (1930), Omaha (1935), War Admiral (1937), Whirlaway (1941), Count Fleet (1943), Assault (1946), Citation (1948), Secretariat (1973), Seattle Slew (1977), and Affirmed (1978).

There is also a Canadian Triple Crown, consisting of the Queen's Plate, the Prince of Wales Stakes and the Breeders' Stakes. The former is a mile and a quarter, and the latter two are a mile and a half. The Argentine Triple Crown consists of the Polla de Potrillos, the Gran Premio Jockey Club, and the Gran Premio Nacional, which are 1600, 2000 and 2500 meters, respectively.

The Japanese Triple Crown includes the Satsuki Shou, Tokyo Yuushun (Tokyo Derby) and the Kikuka Shou, which are 2000, 2400 and 3000 meters, respectively.

The German Triple Crown races are the oldest in continental Europe, having been first run between 1869 and 1881. These races are the Henckel-Rennen at Gelsenkirchen (1600 meters), the Deutsches Derby at Hamburg (2400 meters) and the Deutsches St Leger at Dortmund (2800 meters).

Elsewhere in Europe, specifically in France and Italy, there are tripartite racing events that are de facto 'triple crowns' which are not specifically known or run as such,

Opposite: 'They're off!' sounds the voice over the loudspeaker as a brace of fine Thoroughbreds explodes from the gate.

although they are the equivalent of such triads in Germany and Britain.

In France, the three races are the Poule d'Essai, the Prix du Jockey Club, and the Prix Royal Oak. In Italy, there are the Premio Parioli, the Derby Italiano and the St Leger Italiano.

In Australia, the premier races are the 2050 meter WS Cox Plate, run at Moonee Valley near Melbourne, Victoria, and the 3200 meter Melbourne Cup, held at Flemington, Victoria.

Harness racing had its beginnings around New York and in New England states, and in 1788, a gray Thoroughbred stallion named Messenger, who had been winning races in England, was imported to the United States to stand at stud. Messenger was a gray who traced his heritage to Darley Arabian through Flying Childers. Messenger's descendants had the ability to trot and were specifically bred to enhance that trait. His initial appearance in North America was not noteworthy, but the foals he sired were very fast, natural trotters.

Harness racing gradually developed due to improved tracks, and a lighter racing cart. Improved breeding has, no doubt, had

a part but it is difficult to say just how much. Harness races have not been as widespread as running races. They are engaged in mostly in the Atlantic and midwestern states.

Harness races are for trotters and pacers. The purpose of this selective crossbreeding was to produce superior driving horses, with the accent on racing. By 1789, if a horse qualified by trotting a mile in 2:30 or by pacing the mile in 2:25, the horse was eligible for registration. This way, the 'standard' was established. In the selective breeding of these horses, 'gait begets gait,' with each type of horse producing its own style of movement in their progeny. In the case of the pacer, both legs on one side of the animal move forward at the same time. The horse is usually equipped with a special harness, called a 'pacing hobble,' that discourages any tendency to break into a diagonal trot, or gallop.

Improved breeding led to the Standardbred, which was bred especially for the sport. Standardbreds are not as large as Thoroughbreds, but their long forearms and muscles enable them to extend to great speeds while trotting or pacing. They have

Below: A pair of classic views of Churchill Downs during the running of America's premier race, the Kentucky Derby.
Opposite top and bottom: *Training for a harness race.*

influenced the nature of harness racing all over Europe, as well as in Russia, Australia and New Zealand. Hambletonian, who, as we've noted, was the great sire of the Standardbred, was by Abdallah, by Mambrino, by Messenger. Hambletonian was a big, strong stallion out of a mare with Norfolk trotters in her ancestry and who was foaled in 1849. Indeed all horses of Standardbred breeding have been referred to as 'Hambletonians,' and the most important harness race is also known as the Hambletonian, run each summer at East Rutherford, New Jersey.

In 1988, the trotter Arbro Goal won both heats of this $1,156,800 race. This three-year-old led practically every step of the way in both heats. His time for the first heat was 1:54.6, the fastest time ever recorded for a Hambletonian heat. His time for his second heat was 1:55.4, and again, he set a new

record by trotting the first half mile faster than any horse ever had in the 63 year history of the race. In the first heat, Rule The Wind placed second and Firm Tribute finished third. In the second heat, Shaerpa Kosmas was second and Speedy Crown came in third.

STEEPLECHASE

Steeplechase racing existed in England between about 1825 and 1835, possibly created by a man named John Fromby, and was institutionalized in 1837 with the first official Grand National Steeplechase, which was run with four entrants. In 1838, ten horses entered the race. Sir William, the favorite, was the winner. He was ridden by Captain Becher, who apparently was such an imposing figure that the most famous jump in the race was subsequently named after him. Other early jumps were dubbed Canal Turn, Valentines and Anchor Bridge. There were two dozen jumps in the four mile race (twice around a two mile track). As might be expected, from the beginning the race was dominated by English and Irish horses, with an occasional horse of Scottish ownership capturing top honors.

Time records were not kept until 1863, when records show that the Grand National Steeplechase lasted 11 minutes, 10 seconds. In 1908, an American bred but English-trained 10-year-old named Rubio won in 10 minutes, 3-3/5 seconds. He was ridden by an Englishman named HB Bletsoe weighing 10 stone, 5 pounds. The following year, a horse from France won for the first time. His name was Parliament. His time: 9 minutes, 53-4/5 seconds. This record was tied in 1922 when Music Hall thundered home in first place. In 1933 another American owned, though English bred, horse called Kellsboro Jack came in first. He was owned by Mrs Ambrose Clark.

In 1938, Battleship, the first horse that was owned, bred, and also ridden by an American, was the winner. The smallest horse since The Lamb had covered the course in 1871, Battleship stood only 15.2 hands high. Sired by the famed Thoroughbred Man o' War, he was owned by Mrs Marion Scott and ridden by 17-year-old Bruce Hobbs (11 stone, 6 pounds), the youngest jockey in the history of the race. Before the race was run, the little horse was all but overlooked, as the favorite, Royal Danieli, was so imposing in appearance and considered a sure bet to win. Battleship posted a time of 9 minutes, 29-4/5 seconds, in his record-breaking run.

Steeplechase jumping originated with structures built on racetracks. The tradition of using horses for riding, cavalry, racing and hunting goes back for centuries. However, competition which involved jumping over structures made specifically for this purpose dates back less than a century. Many horses will not take to jumping, and if a horse does not naturally enjoy jumping there is little chance that it can ever be used in jumping sports. On the other hand, there are those that seem to have a natural aptitude for it and enjoy it as much as running. However, Thoroughbreds compose the majority of top jumping horses with heights in the 17 hands range.

France pioneered the development of steeplechase jumping, with Henry Leclerc being the top rider. He won many national and European championships, but was killed during the German invasion of his country in 1940.

Jumping events at today's meets consist of a rider guiding his horse through a set pattern of jumps over a timed course, with 'faults' given as penalties for mistakes. Faults may be incurred when the horse either refuses a jump or knocks down a bar during a jump. Jumping has been an Olympic event since 1912, and today, there are also world championship events, with points building toward international grand championship meets. Points are given in accordance with how a horse places at each of the individual meets, a system similar to that used in Grand Prix auto racing.

Below: *Clearing the hurdle in perfect form.* **Opposite:** *The horse performs beautifully as the rider is in deep concentration during formal competition.*

Because of his interest in horse sporting events, Baron de Coubertin, then president of the Olympic Committee, encouraged Count Clarence von Rosen, master of horse events to the king of Sweden, to make equestrian events part of the 1906 Olympic games. However, they were not included until 1912. At that time, ten nations sent 62 horses and 71 riders to compete. Russia entered with seven horses and riders, and the United States with four of each, including George Patton, who later achieved fame as an American general. Great Britain had four riders and five horses. The program included the 'Three Day Event,' also called the 'Military,' which was open only to officers on active duty. There was also a 'Steeplechase' event. Under the exceedingly stringent rules of the time, riders were eliminated quite quickly. Sweden made a clean sweep of medals in individual dressage, with their top competitor being Lt Nordlander. Captain Cariou on Migson

Below: Britain's Princess Anne, an accomplished rider, has participated in many major equestrian events, such as the European Championships, as seen here.
Opposite: A perfect jump is a joy indeed!

116

Below: Coming over the hurdle.

Opposite bottom: *Training for Steeplechase is an exacting and time-consuming activity, but the rewards are great.*

and Count Bonde on Emperior also captured gold medals in this event.

At the beginning of the twentieth century, high jumping was already an established, popular sport throughout the world. Steeplechase events, and the less strenuous 'Hunter Class' event, are now held all over the world, with the Grand National Steeplechase, still held in Aintree, England, being the most widely known as well as the most exciting and grueling of these races. It consists of going twice around a two mile course, with two dozen difficult jumps, the most famous of which is Becher's Brook. Both this steeplechase and the Becher's Brook jump were immortalized in the 1944 film *National Velvet*, starring a teenage Elizabeth Taylor.

RODEO

Rodeos are modern-day sporting events that evolved from the contests of skill among ranch hands in the nineteenth century. The word rodeo, derived from the Spanish, literally means the rounding up of cattle. At the end of the early roundups, the cowboys would wager among themselves and compete for awards. These contests were based on features that characterized the cowboy's daily work and included bronc riding, roping, racing and cutting contests.

Soon, the rodeos began to attract people from other ranches, which, in turn, attracted the attention of people with an eye for prof-

Below: A Quarter Horse and cowboy in action at the Pioneer Days Rodeo in Guymon, Oklahoma.
Opposite: Training for the barrel race event.

it. One such entrepreneur was William 'Buffalo Bill' Cody, whose Wild West Show was internationally renowned in the 1890s. He combined rodeo and circus events, and his show toured North America with cowboys, Native Americans, horses, and celebrities such as Chief Sitting Bull of the Sioux nation.

The Miller Brothers of Oklahoma, with their 101 Ranch Show, carried on in a similar manner. Such wild west shows toured the country, and in 1896, a well planned and successful rodeo was held in Denver, Colorado. The following year it was held in Cheyenne, Wyoming, where it has been held

ever since. From then on rodeos became more of a fixed event and have been held at the same places year after year. The dates became fixed and are guided mostly by the season. The season generally culminates in the autumn with the Grand National in San Francisco and the National Finals — the Super Bowl of Rodeo — in Las Vegas. A few shows, such as these final events of the season, as well as those held at Madison Square Garden and Fort Worth, are indoor rodeos.

Among the other important events of the season are Cheyenne Frontier Days, the Pendleton Round-Up and the Calgary Stampede which is Canada's premier rodeo. Thousands of people travel west to see them each year. But the rodeo may also be seen in many small towns of the Midwest and East. They have greatly influenced the attitudes and opinions of the people of the East towards the people of the West. Today, the rodeo is a national feature and a majority of the people have a desire to see one of the big ones.

The champions of various rodeo events are determined by the number of dollars won from the rodeo purses. The contestant who wins the most points in one event is declared the champion of that event, and the contes-

Below: *A saddle bronc with obvious draft horse ancestry attempts to throw a cowboy at the National Finals Rodeo.* **Opposite:** *A well-trained Quarter Horse stands by as the cowboy wrestles with a calf.*

tant winning the most points in all events is declared the all-around champion. There are various rodeo events and variations of the same events. Some events are based on the time it takes to perform the event in a satisfactory manner. Other events are based on the manner of performing in a given amount of time.

As late as the 1940s, few rodeo contestants could depend entirely upon the rodeo for their means of living, and the majority were ranch hands who took time off from their regular ranch work to compete. In the late 1950s, this began to change. Jim Shoulders, who was the World Champion All-Around Cowboy from 1956 through 1959, was rodeo's first superstar. Larry Mahan and Tom Ferguson, who were the World Champion All-Around Cowboys for a dozen years between them in the 1960s and 1970s, became stars on the level of those at the top of any other major professional sports.

Bucking horse riding, or bronc riding, is the most spectacular rodeo event to most people. It is dangerous, hard on the rider, and is generally indulged in by the younger people, although some people ride for many years.

Early rodeos, and the great riders who competed against one another in them, never would have come about had it not been for great bucking horses, or saddle broncs. These horses are generally of mixed breed, with Quarter Horse and various draft horse blood (particularly that of the Percheron). Few western horsemen have not heard of CB Irwin's Steamboat, who started bucking off the best rodeo riders in Wyoming late in the nineteenth century, and it is he who is commemorated in silhouette on the license plate of that state. It is said that he never failed to do his best to throw his riders, and he succeeded a majority of the time.

Bronc riding is done with a plain halter, one rein and an association saddle having a 14

Below: Rodeo probably originated in the Texas-Mexico border country, but today it is an international sport, with rodeos taking place in Australia as well as North America. This Australian cowboy is riding a Waler, a saddle breed that was developed in Australia.

Opposite: *A convict cowboy hangs on for dear life at the McAlester, Oklahoma Prison Rodeo.*

to 15-inch tree. The rein is three or four strand grass or cotton rope not over one inch in diameter. It must not be wrapped around the hand. One hand holds the rein and the rider must not change hands on the rein. The hand holding the rein must be held above the horses neck as he leaves the chute. The rider may cinch the saddle or examine it before he rides. The horse must be spurred the first jump out of the chute and the rider continues to spur throughout the ride. Where three judges are used, one will score the horse and two the rider. The three figures are added together to determine the total score. If a horse fails to buck sufficiently or anything happens which is not the fault of the rider that prevents him from having a chance to exhibit his skill, the judges may give him a re-ride.

In bareback bronc riding, the horse is ridden with only a single rope tied around the horse's flank girth. The rigging has a D ring for a hand hold similar to the one used on horses. The rules are that one hand will be used on the rigging. If the rider is knocked off at the chute, the horse falls, or fails to buck, the rider will be entitled to a re-ride. The horse must be spurred in the shoulder the first jump out of the chute.

Below: A wild ride at the National Finals Rodeo.
Opposite: A team in harness pulling a stagecoach at the Cherokee Strip Celebration. Stagecoaches are a popular means of evoking the spirit of the Old West.
Overleaf: This handsome little Pinto colt is a newcomer to the world.

Index